WEEKEND WARRIORS

SET LIST ONE

MINUS DRUMS

7161

MUSIC MINUS ONE
DRUMS

7161

CONTENTS

*Please note that prefatory material for each song may appear after the related chart to preserve comfortable page-turns.

ISBN 1-59615-857-3

Hey, whatever happened to that bass player we knew in school?
Gary was a great guitar player—I wonder if he is still playing?
I heard that President Clinton was a sax player—does he do gigs now that he is out of a day job?

There are millions of musicians who don't make their living playing their instruments. Many of these folks have an unbridled passion for music and performing—they just happen to do something else—but they are really musicians at their core. When the weekend rolls around, it is incredible how many of these teachers, doctors, lawyers, civil servants, etc. plug in or climb behind the drum kit and launch into their favorite songs in a venue near you. We call those musicians "weekend warriors." I can go to my social-network pages at any time and find out where my doctor, or the owner of my favorite music retailer, are performing. They take music seriously, and believe me, many of them are great players—they just chose to make music an important hobby instead of their profession. Earlier this year, I taught at a great bass camp in Nashville. Every student at that camp was a weekend warrior. I asked the group, "what do you want to accomplish as a bass player?" Expecting to be met with answers demanding I turn them into the next Jaco or Victor Wooten, I was encouraged by the responses. Warren, a manager in the Florida Health Department gave me the answer that inspired this book. He said, "we want to be able to go play a gig, to know the songs that all the bands play, and to be able to perform them." He then gave me some song requests, all of which I knew by heart. I have taken that for granted for so long. So these books are for Warren, and all the players like him.

This is NOT a karaoke project. We record karaoke or background tracks for this company every week. We spend a huge amount of time to try to faithfully recreate every part of a record. It is not unusual to have 6 tracks of guitars, 6 passes of keyboards, multiple percussion passes, as well as 10-20 tracks of background vocals. What does that mean to you? It means that if you go to a weekend gig with a 5 piece band, you are going to have to condense those things and find a way to perform the signature grooves, lines, riffs, and rhythm tracks. That is what the "Weekend Warrior" series will do for you. We are true to the original tempo, key, and parts. In songs where there are multiple guitar or keyboard parts, we will demonstrate how to pick out the most important parts to be true to the song. Each book is customized for the individual instrument with instruction on determining those parts. You will find the signature parts of each song notated along with helpful hints on everything from sounds to style. Each song will also have a complete chord chart with measure numbers so that we can help you find where the licks happen in context. We are going to be borrowing from the set lists of working bands around the country as well as your requests to bring you future volumes. I have been asked how many songs I know. I have no idea. I have played in a society band that had a 400 song set list—and that is a fraction of what I know. More importantly—within the musicians creating this series for you, that number is incredibly high. But the goal here is to give the "weekend warrior" the repertoire to be able to sit in with most any band, to handle common requests, and to ultimately start creating their own set lists.

For most of us, the true joy of music is sharing it. While there are millions of musicians "jamming" in their basements with headphones and an audience of the family pet, the true experience is walking into a venue and playing songs that put people on the dance-floor or at least put a lot of smiles on their faces as they sing along. This series is a wonderful tool to help facilitate that—whether you are a teenager wanting to figure out how to make some gas money on weekends, to a working band that wants to actually capture the essence of the original hits—Weekend Warrior Set List is for you. For the individual musician, this helps make you marketable and useful. For an entire band, this becomes a perfect rehearsal tool to put the whole band on the same page. ENJOY!!!

Brown Eyed Girl

Brown Eyed Girl is one of the greatest "hippie" era anthems. Although there are hundreds of versions of what Van Morrison's lyrics actually are saying, the song became a hit for its infectious groove and the band and audience sing-along section. This track was cut in New York and features some great studio musicians in a different environment than normal. This record sounds like a party, and that is the prime reason that you are going to play this every time the party is starting to drag.

This is a classic "push beat" groove, meaning that beat 3 on the bass drum part is anticipated throughout. In the second verse, the ride cymbal is added on the "and of two." This also happens in the third verse. In a live situation, you should play the 2 and 4 tambourine part on the intro on your hi-hat if there is no percussionist.

Here is the pattern for verse 1

Here is the pattern for verse 2

Brown Eyed Girl

As Recorded by Van Morrison

Words and Music by
Van Morrison

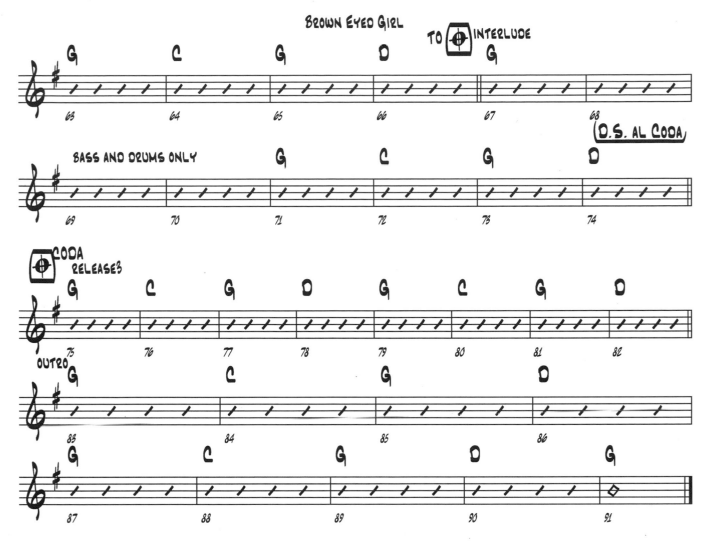

Hey where did we go, days when the rains came
Down in the hollow, playin' a new game
Laughing and a running hey, hey, skipping and a jumping
In the misty morning fog with our hearts a thumpin' and you
My brown eyed girl, you my brown eyed girl

Whatever happened to Tuesday and so slow
Going down the old mine with a transistor radio
Standing in the sunlight laughing, hiding behind a rainbow's wall
Slipping and sliding all along the waterfall with you
My brown eyed girl, you my brown eyed girl

Do you remember when, we used to sing
Shalalalalalalalalalalaladeeda, shalalalalalalalalalalaladeeda, ladeeda

So I had to find my way, now that I'm on my own
Saw you just the other day, and my how you have grown

Cast my memory back there Lord, I'm overcome thinking about
Making love in the green grass behind the stadium with you
My brown eyed girl, you my brown eyed girl
Do you remember when, we used to sing
Shalalalalalalalalalalaladeeda, shalalalalalalalalalalaladeeda, ladeeda
Shalalalalalalalalalalaladeeda, shalalalalalalalalalalaladeeda, ladeeda

Margaritaville

As recorded by Jimmy Buffet

Words and Music by
Jimmy Buffett

MARGARITAVILLE

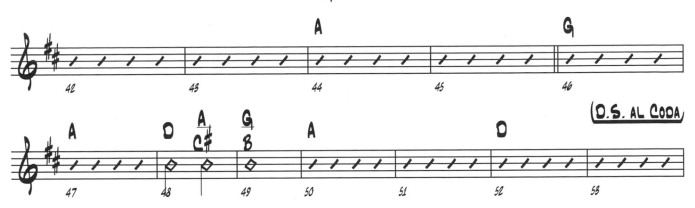

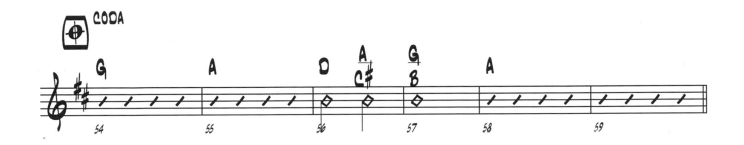

Nibblin' on spongecake, watchin' the sun bake
All of those tourists covered with oil
Strummin my six-string on my front porch swing
Smell those shrimp, they're beginning to boil

CHORUS:
Wasting away again in Margaritaville
searchin for my lost shaker of salt
Some people claim that there's a woman to blame
but I know, its nobody's fault

Don't know the reason, I stayed here all season
got nothing to show but this brand new tattoo
but its a real beauty, a Mexican cutie
how it got here I haven't a clue

CHORUS

I blew out my flip flop, stepped on a pop top
cut my heal had to cruise on back home
but there's booze in the blender and soon it will render
that frozen concoction that helps me hang on

CHORUS

Margaritaville

Jimmy Buffet's "Margaritaville" is truly an anthem for the "laid back in the summertime" attitude. Whether you are in Key West or Seattle, when a warm breeze comes your way, you can bet "Margaritaville" is being played by a band or single next to the tiki bar! This track was originally produced by Norbert Putnam, a Nashville session bassist and producer at Criteria Studios in Miami. Nashville great Kenneth Buttrey played drums on the track, but most of the musicians were part of Buffet's Coral Reefer Band. The use of steel drums and marimba contribute to the "island feel" of the track.

This has a very basic drum groove with Buttrey on drums and the late Farrell Morris on percussion. For live, you might play a tom tom part on the chorus as part of the drum groove to cover a bit of the conga part.

Intro and Verse:

For chorus-do the same thing but use full snare.

Chorus alternative:

Mony Mony

"Mony Mony" is a classic rock song from the "psychedelic" era. While many people have wondered who was Mony, the truth is the songwriters were looking out the window of the office where they were writing in New York. Across the way was the flashing sign for the giant bank, Mutual of New York---MONY. Oh well, every song isn't inspired by a Shakespeare sonnet. The success of this song was probably based on the simple hook and the fact that you could sing along after one listen. This song is right at the top of a male tenor range, so don't be surprised if this winds up in G or even in A. Learn the relationships between the chords—you should be able to play a song like "Mony Mony" in any key.

This song has a basic groove with a couple of variations.

Intro and verse:

Build-up into chorus or pre-chorus:

Breakdown "boogaloo":

Mony Mony

Words and Music by Bobby Bloom,
Tommy James, Ritchie Cordell and
Bo Gentry

As performed by Tommy James and The Shondells

Mony Mony

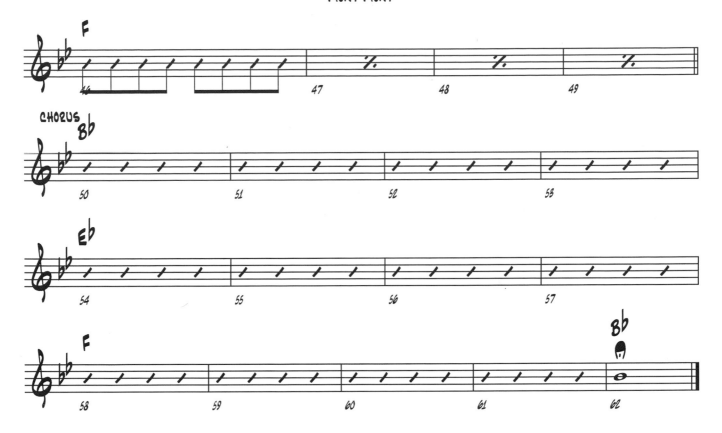

Here she come now, say Mony Mony
Well shoot 'em down, turn around come home Mony
Hey she gives me love and I feel alright now
You got me tossin', turnin' in the middle of the night
And I feel alright, I say yeah
Yeah, yeah, yeah, yeah

CHORUS:
Well you make me feel, so, good, yeah
 So good, yeah, come on, alright, I say yeah
Yeah, yeah, yeah, yeah

Break me, shake me, Mony Mony
Shotgun, get it done, come on Mony
Don't stop cookin', it feels so good, yeah
Hey, well don't stop now, hey come on Mony
Come on Mony, I say yeah
Yeah, yeah, yeah, yeah

CHORUS

Mustang Sally
As Recorded By Wilson Pickett

Words and Music by
Bonny Rice

MUSTANG SALLY

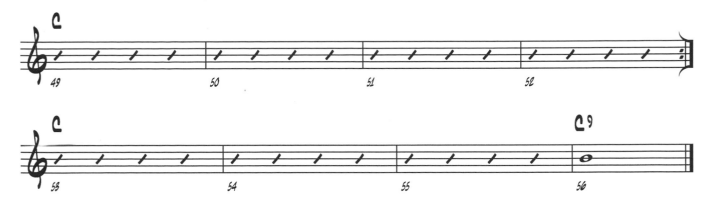

Mustang Sally, guess you better slow your mustang down.
Mustang Sally, guess you better slow your mustang down.
You been running all over the town now.
Oh! I guess I'll have to put your flat feet on the ground.
What I say, now listen

CHORUS:
All you want to do is ride around Sally, (ride, Sally, ride).
All you want to do is ride around Sally, (ride, Sally, ride).
All you want to do is ride around Sally, (ride, Sally, ride).
All you want to do is ride around Sally, (ride, Sally, ride).
One of these early mornings, oh, you gonna be wiping your weeping eyes.

I bought you a brand new mustang 'bout nineteen sixty five
Now you come around,signifying woman, you don't wanna let me ride.
Mustang Sally, guess you better slow that mustang down.
You been running all over the town
Oh! I guess I'll have to put your flat feet on the ground.

CHORUS

Mustang Sally

Wilson Pickett recorded "Mustang Sally" in 1967 in Muscle Shoals, AL, a hotbed for soul and R&B recording. There is probably not another song that has been played as many times in bars as this soul classic, a tribute to not only the Ford Mustang, but to summertime and fun. Pickett's soulful voice along with the huge groove created by the amazing musicians make this an all-time great recording, as well as one of the songs that lights a fire in a party!

This is Muscle Shoals at its best. It is the same hypnotic groove throughout, with minor variations. Note the beat displacement trick in the sixth measure of the second chorus. Whew!

Here is our basic groove:

My Girl

"My Girl" is a wonderful example of the incredible production value of Motown recordings during the 1960's. The track builds from the beginning, just bass and kick drum, then a single note guitar is added, then an accent guitar, and finally the iconic orchestration. The whole approach is patient and exactly right. As a "live" song, "My Girl" never fails to strike the right chord with a crowd as long as you remain faithful to the song's approach.

This track is quintessential Motown, with Benny Benjamin on drums. It starts with bass drum only. Finger snaps enter on measure 3. You could play closed hi-hat where the finger snaps enter. Also note the recurring Motown fill. There are a couple of variations, so learn them all!

Intro:

Verse:

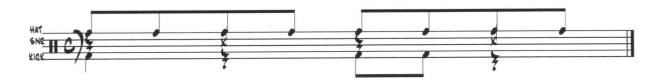

Pre-chorus:

MMO 7161

My Girl

As Recorded By The Temptations

Words and Music by
William "Smokey" Robinson
and Ronald White

My Girl

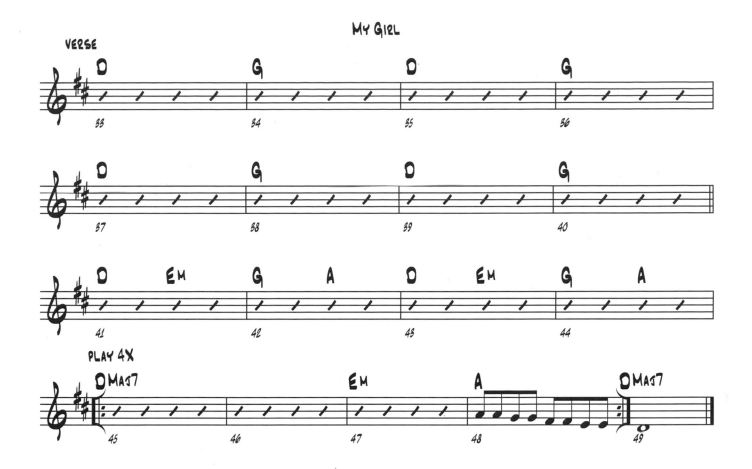

I've got sunshine on a cloudy day
When it's cold outside, I've got the month of May

CHORUS:
Well, I guess you'll say
What can make me feel this way?
My Girl (my girl, my girl)
Talkin' bout my girl (My girl)

I've got so much honey the bees envy me
I've got a sweeter song than the birds in the trees

CHORUS

I don't need no money, fortune, or fame
I've got all the riches baby, one man can claim

CHORUS

MMO 7161

Old Time Rock and Roll

As Recorded By Bob Seger and the Silver Bullet Band

Words and Music by
George Jackson and
Thomas E. Jones III

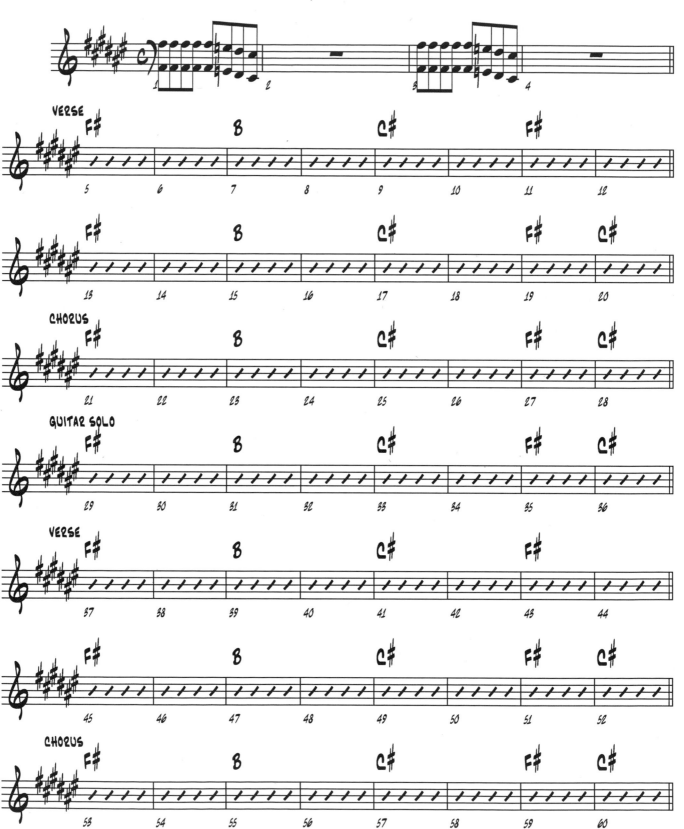

OLD TIME ROCK AND ROLL

Just take those old records off the shelf	Won't go to hear 'em play a tango
I'll sit and listen to them by myself	I'd rather hear some blues or funky old soul
Today's music ain't got the same soul	There's only one sure way to get me to go
I like that old time rock and roll	Start playing old time rock and roll
Don't even take me to a disco	Call me a relic, call me what you will
You'll never even get me out on the floor	Say I'm old fashioned, say I'm over the hill
In ten minutes I'll be late for the door	Today's music ain't got the same soul
I like that old time rock and roll	I like that old time rock and roll

CHORUS:
Still like that old time rock and roll
That kind of music just soothes my soul
I reminisce about the days of old
With that old time rock and roll

CHORUS

Old Time Rock and Roll

All it takes is 8 descending piano notes. Those 8 notes are traditionally followed by the screams of the audience for they know "Old Time Rock and Roll" is cranking up. Bob Seger went to Muscle Shoals to get a taste of the soulful musicians there, and this hit was one of the successes of that group of sessions. I personally know 3 different piano players claiming to be the "guy" on that track—so the mystery lives on. Regardless of who played on this track, it is a slamming 3 chord rock anthem. With the drummer back there "chopping wood," the boogie woogie guitar and piano and the rock solid thump of the bass, Bob had a great bed over which to deliver this classic vocal. This song is pitched high—and it works great up there, but don't be surprised to have the band leader call this song in D or E (that is to keep the vocalist from applying for a job at the post office!)

This track has the basic "four on the floor" groove. It is still an effective groove in popular music. It is constant throughout with an occasional added part on the snare drum.

Here is the basic groove:

Here is a variation in the solo:

Soul Man

"Soul Man" certainly ranks as an all-time classic R&B track. From the original Sam and Dave recording through The Blues Brothers, this song just drips soul. This is a great example of Memphis recording, incredible bass and drum groove with Cropper and Booker T putting the icing on the cake. Unfortunately, this song has been hijacked by society bands and Vegas show groups and turned into a high energy show piece. The real magic of this track is the interplay between the instruments, and the tempo is absolutely the cornerstone of the groove.

This is Memphis's Stax Records Band with Al Jackson Jr. on drums. There are three different grooves on this track.

Intro groove:

Verse groove:

Chorus groove:

Note the 4 quarter notes on the snare drum in the first measure of the second chorus.

Soul Man

As Recorded by Sam and Dave

Words and Music by
Isaac Hayes and David Porter

Soul Man

Comin' to ya on a dusty road
Good lovin, I got a truck load
And when you get it, you got something
So don't worry, cause I'm coming

CHORUS:
I'm a soul man
I'm a soul man
I'm a soul man
I'm a soul man

Got what I got the hard way
And I'll make it better each and every day
So honey don't you fret
Cause you ain't seen nothing yet

CHORUS

I was brought up on a side street
I learned how to love before I could eat
I was educated from good stock
When I start loving, I just can't stop

CHORUS

BRIDGE:
Well grab the rope and I'll pull you in
Give you hope and be your only boyfriend
Yeah, yeah, yeah, yeah

CHORUS

Stand By Me

As Recorded by Ben E. King

Words and Music by
Jerry Leiber, Mike Stoller
and Ben E. King

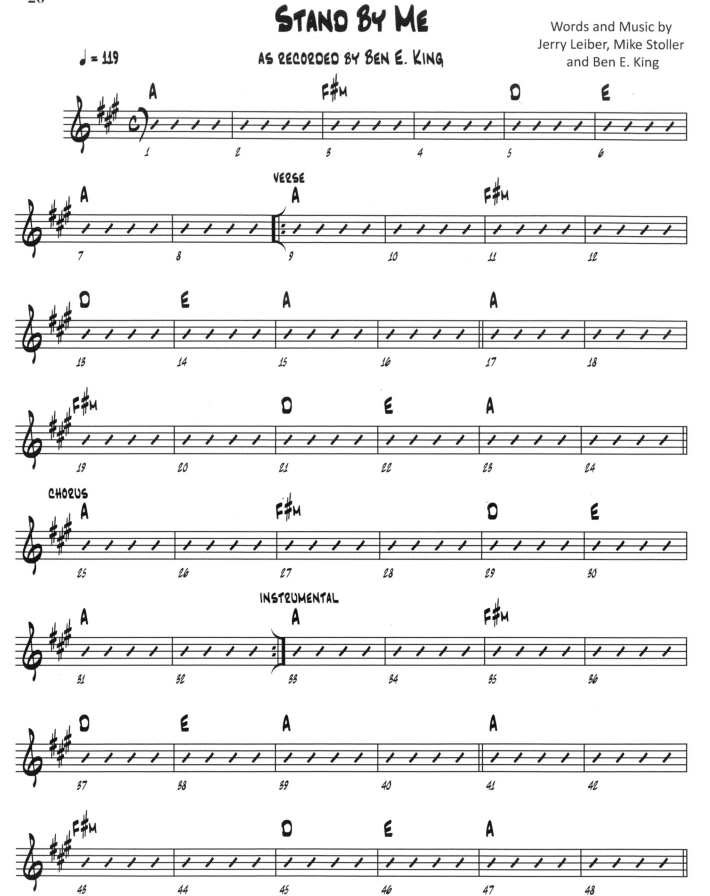

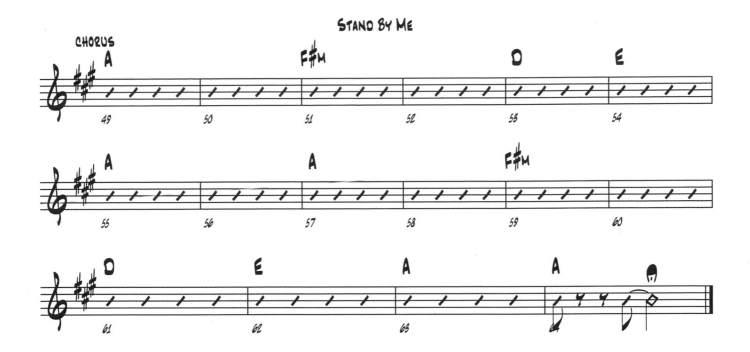

STAND BY ME

When the night has come, and the land is dark
And the moon is the only light we'll see
No I won't be afraid, oh I won't be afraid
Just as long as you stand, stand by me

CHORUS:
So darling, darling
Stand by me, oh stand by me
Oh stand, stand by me, stand by me

If the sky that we look upon should tumble and fall
And the mountains should crumble to the sea
I won't cry, I won't cry, no I won't shed a tear
Just as long as you stand, stand by me

CHORUS

Stand By Me

"Stand By Me" is a truly unique song. Four simple chords, a moderate tempo, no drums—yet it has become a standard in American pop and soul music. Ben. E King's incredibly soulful delivery, tasteful groove playing, and a classic string arrangement have contributed to the songs original success, and more recent successes in film and television uses.

The drum part on this track is almost non-existent. It is almost all a simple percussion part. My suggestion is to play a simple drum part with the bass drum following the bass.

Intro: You could play hi-hat in place of guiro and cymbal instead of triangle.

This is a suggestion for the verse:

This is a suggestion for the chorus:

Sweet Caroline

I can't imagine anyone expected a "schmaltzy" pop song to become a party anthem, but "Sweet Caroline" did just that. Whether you are playing a frat party or a society blowout, this song has to be on the set list. The original track by Neil Diamond was a big hit, and it just never seemed to go away. This track is quite different than some of our other choices for this project. This is a "big-budget" Hollywood session, with top recording musicians at every spot.

This is an orchestrated session and the drummer is reading a part. All sections are uniquely different from the others. The eighth notes are played with a swing (triplet) feel.

Intro:

Verse:

Pre-chorus:

Chorus:

Sweet Caroline

As Recorded by Neil Diamond

Words and Music by
Neil Diamond

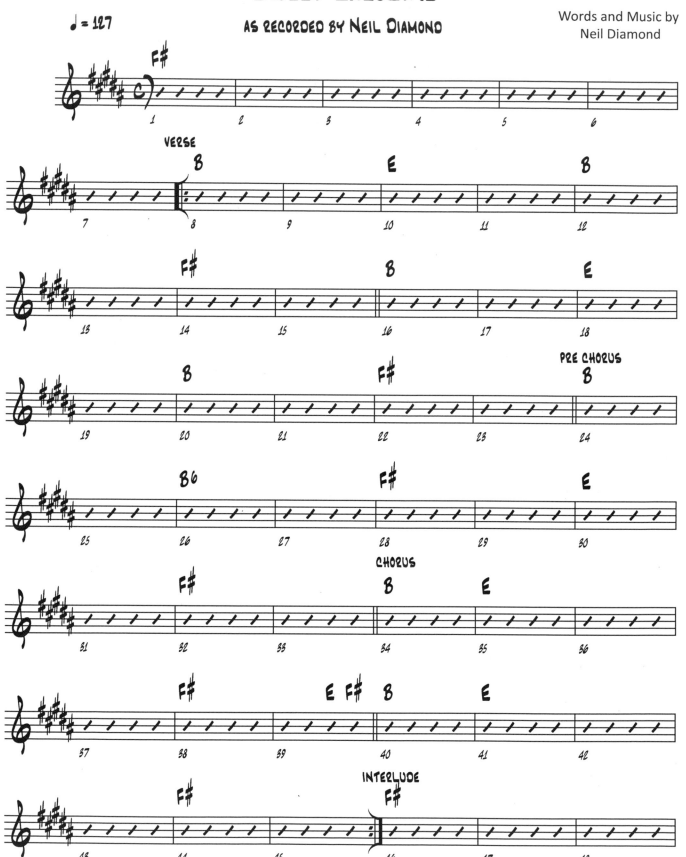

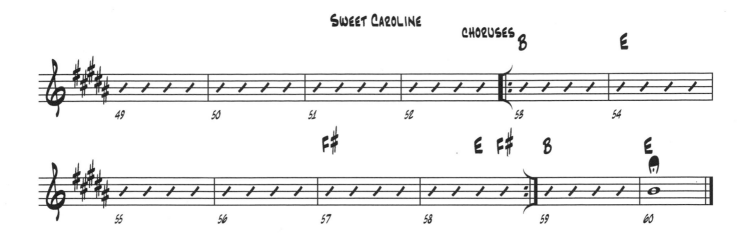

Where it began, I can't begin to knowin'
But then I know it's growing strong
Was in the spring, and spring became the summer
Who'd have believed you'd come along
Hands, touchin' hands, reachin' out, touchin' me, touchin' you

CHORUS:
Sweet Caroline, good times never seemed so good
I've been inclined to believe they never would, but now I

Look at the night, and it don't seem so lonely
We fill it up with only two
And when I hurt, hurtin' runs off my shoulders
How can I hurt when I'm with you
Warm, touching warm, reachin' out, touchin' me, touchin' you

CHORUS

Under the Boardwalk

As Recorded By The Drifters

Words and Music by
Artie Resnick and Kenny Young

Under the Boardwalk

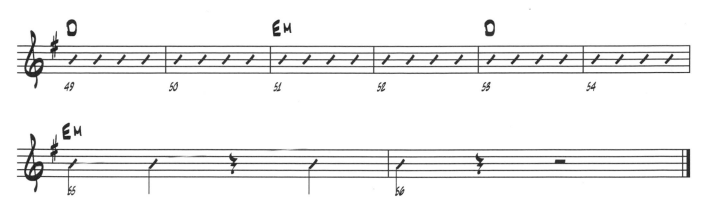

Oh when the sun beats down and burns the tar up on the roof
And your shoes get so hot, you wish your tired feet were fireproof
Under the boardwalk, down by the sea
On a blanket with my baby is where I'll be

CHORUS:
Under the boardwalk out of the sun
Under the boardwalk we'll be having some fun
Under the boardwalk people walking above
Under the boardwalk we'll be falling in love
Under the boardwalk, boardwalk

From the park you hear the happy sounds of a carousel
And you can almost taste the hot dogs and French fries they sell
Under the boardwalk, down by the sea
On a blanket with my baby is where I'll be

CHORUS

Oh, under the boardwalk, down by the sea
On a blanket with my baby is where I'll be

CHORUS

MMO 7161

Under the Boardwalk

While "Under the Boardwalk" reached hit status in its initial release by The Drifters, it has had a long and healthy life as a classic song in the "beach music" genre. There is a dance that dominates that music called "The Shag," and tens of thousands of dancers, young and not so young have Shagged to this classic. In the south, this is a standard. From the great bass line and percussion to the string arrangement—this song is very special, and will never fail you on a gig!

This is a simple drum part, but has two percussionists playing too. In a live situation, you could cover the guiro and triangle parts in the intro by playing on the closed hi-hat and cymbal bell.

Verse groove:

Bridge groove:

WEEKEND WARRIORS STUDIO BAND

TIM SMITH is a very busy bassist and producer in Nashville. He received a degree in studio music and jazz from the University of Miami in 1979. Upon graduation, he moved to Nashville at the request of legendary producer and Monument Records founder, Fred Foster. Within a few months Tim had appeared on top hits by Tom Jones, Willie Nelson, Dolly Parton, Kris Kristoferson and many others. After stints in Los Angeles and Paris, Tim returned to Nashville in 1996. At that time he began performing and producing saxophone legend Boots Randolph (all of which are available as releases with Music Minus One). Tim's credits are as diverse as anyone in Music City, ranging from country legends to jazz saxophonist Bill Evans, former Kansas lead singer John Elefante and many others.

RODDY SMITH has been performing for over 35 years. Through rock, country, or jazz, he has become one of the most versatile guitarists on the scene. He has recorded and performed with artists like Boots Randolph, Johnny Cash, Joe Sample, Bill Evans, The Moody Brothers, Radney Foster and many others. Like his brother Tim, they have recorded extensively with their band Mr. Groove, including acclaimed projects with Bonnie Bramlett.

BOBBY OGDIN, our keyboardist, is an icon in Nashville recording history. He has been a mainstay in the studio scene since the 70's, playing on major hits for Travis Tritt, Neil McCoy, Clay Walker and Ronnie Milsap. Perhaps Bobby is best known for his tasteful piano work on all of The Judds' recordings. He has performed live with artists as diverse as Ray Price, Ween, Lynn Anderson and the Marshall Tucker Band. He was also a member of Elvis Presley's band.

TOMMY WELLS got his start in recording in Detroit at the "mother church" of soul music, Motown Records. He moved to Nashville in the 70's and has been one of the top drummers in town ever since. Tommy has played on #1 hits by Foster and Lloyd and Ricky Van Shelton. He has recorded extensively with legends like Porter Wagoner, Ray Price, and soul giant Jimmy Hall.

DARRYL JOHNSON, PAT CRAY, AND COREY CRAY are the vocalists on this project. Darryl has been one of the most recorded singers in the karaoke industry, appearing on hundreds of songs, from soul to country, with a big dose of rock thrown in. He currently lives and records in Nashville for clients all around the globe, along with his stunning vocals on the Detroit Memphis Experience projects. Pat is a native of Charlotte, and has long been one of the most in-demand singers and musicians in the region. His son Corey is an up and coming young artist based in Los Angeles and Nashville. He was a host on the Cartoon Network program "Fried Dynamite" and has also been a performer on Broadway. He is currently working with Tim and Roddy Smith on a debut recording.

MUSIC MINUS ONE
50 Executive Boulevard
Elmsford, New York 10523-1325
800-669-7464 (U.S.)/914-592-1188 (International)

www.musicminusone.com
e-mail: info@musicminusone.com

MMO 7161